MANATEES

Printed in China

02 03 04 05 06 5 4 3 2 1

Library of Congress Cataloging-in-Publication Data
Powell, James
Manatees : natural history & conservationn / James Powell.
p. cm. – (Worldlife Library)
Summary: Discusses the evolution, movement, habitat, and physical description
of manatees and dugongs, as well as what can be done to protect them.
ISBN 0-89658-583-2 (pbk.: alk. paper)
1. Sirenia – Juvenile literature. [1. Manatees. 2. Dugong.
3. Endangered species.] I. Title. II Series: Worldlife Library
QL737.S6P68 2002
599.55 – dc21

2002007540

Distributed in Canada by Raincoast Books, 9050 Shaughnessy Street, Vancouver, B.C. V6P 6E5
Published by Voyageur Press, Inc.
123 North Second Street, P.O. Box 338, Stillwater, MN 55082 U.S.A.
651-430-2210, fax 651-430-2211
books@voyageurpress.com   www.voyageurpress.com

Educators, fundraisers, premium and gift buyers, publicists, and marketing managers:
Looking for creative products and new sales ideas? Voyageur Press books are available at special discounts when purchased in quantities,
and special editions can be created to your specifications. For details contact the marketing department at 800-888-9653.

Photographs © 2002 by

Front cover © François Gohier/Ardea London Ltd.
Back cover © Fred Bavendam/Still Pictures
Page 1 © Kennan Ward
Page 4 © Doug Perrine/Seapics.com
Page 6 © Tui de Roy/Minden Pictures
Page 7 © Robert Henno/Still Pictures
Page 9 © Colin Baxter
Page 11 © Doug Perrine/Seapics.com
Page 12 © Doug Perrine/Seapics.com
Page 15 left © Tobias Bernhard/Oxford Scientific Films
Page 15 right © Phillip Colla
Page 16 © Doug Perrine/Seapics.com
Page 19 © David Fleetham/Tom Stack & Associates
Page 20 © Doug Perrine/Seapics.com
Page 23 © Fred Bavendam/Minden Pictures
Page 24 © Doug Perrine/Seapics.com
Page 26 © U.S. Geological Survey, Florida Caribbean Science Center, Sirenian Project
Page 28 © David Fleetham/Tom Stack & Associates
Page 31 © Doug Perrine/Seapics.com
Page 33 © Doug Perrine/Seapics.com

Page 34 © Jeff Foott/Nature Picture Library
Page 37 © Jurgen Freund/Nature Picture Library
Page 38 © François Gohier
Page 40 © Doug Perrine/Seapics.com
Page 42 © Doug Perrine/Seapics.com
Page 45 © Francois Gohier
Page 46 © Colin Baxter
Page 49 © Doc White/Nature Picture Library
Page 50 © Colin Baxter
Page 52 left © Tom and Therisa Stack
Page 52 right © Tom and Therisa Stack
Page 55 © Phillip Colla
Page 56 © Doc White/Ardea London Ltd.
Page 59 © David Fleetham/Tom Stack & Associates
Page 61 © D Parer and E Parer-Cook/Ardea London Ltd.
Page 62 © Kurt Amsler/Ardea London Ltd.
Page 65 top © Jeff Foott/Nature Picture Library
Page 65 bottom © Fred Bavendam/Minden Pictures
Page 66 © Fred Bavendam/Minden Pictures
Page 69 © François Gohier

MANATEES

James Powell

WORLDLIFE
LIBRARY

Voyageur Press

Contents

Introduction

When I was about five or six years old, my father and I were fishing very early one morning in the clear, spring-fed headwaters of Crystal River on the west coast of Florida. The water was warm but the air was cool. Wisps of mist spiraled up through the moss-covered trees. We were sitting there very quietly when a slight movement and swirl on the surface of the water caught my father's attention. He leaned

over to me and whispered, 'Stay still'. He then told me to slowly poke my head over the side of the boat and to look down. What I saw has stuck with me for some 40-odd years. I can still see the image vividly in my mind's eye. Below our little boat was a monster of gigantic proportions, its ghostly gray shape slowly and silently gliding between the cathedrals of waterweeds. My father had no need to tell me to be quiet, I'm not sure I was breathing. It was a 'sea cow', he told me in his southern drawl, or a 'manatee'. He also said that, though he loved to fish, he had only seen a few in his life. He explained that they weren't dangerous, but if I wasn't still they would tip the boat over. He kept emphasizing the 'still' part.

Since that day, these unique and mysterious creatures have held a tremendous fascination for me. surely had no idea that understanding sea cows, learning about their biology, striving for their conservation and following them to some of the most remote places on earth would become my life's work.

My next encounter came a few years later and not far from where I had seen my first manatee.

A female West Indian manatee and her yearling calf glide through the clear waters of a Florida spring.

But this time I thought I was a bit braver. I donned a mask and snorkel and decided to slip into the water to get a better look. With as much stealth as I could conjure, I tried to slide quietly into the water. As I did, the manatee took one look at me and did a head-under somersault. There was a great eruption of spray and water, and I quickly catapulted myself out of the water back to the safety of my boat, very sure that I had narrowly escaped certain death. Back in the early 1960s, few people even knew of the existence of manatees in Crystal River and certainly no one, or so I believed at the time, had lived to tell about swimming with one.

That year, my life's direction became fixed when I had the fortunate opportunity to meet Daniel S. Hartman. 'Woody', as he was called, had arrived in Crystal River in 1967 to be the first biologist to conduct an in-depth study of sea cows in their natural habitat. He was working on his Ph.D. from Cornell University in New York. I was just a young teenager growing up in coastal Florida. After observing this stranger canvassing 'my' river for about a month, wondering what he was doing and curious about the strange name, 'Trichechus', he had dubbed his bathtub boat, I decided to approach him one day and ask him what he was doing on 'my' river.

It didn't take long for both of us to discover that we had little in common, but we could work out an arrangement whereby he could help satiate my curiosity about manatees and I would teach him how to navigate through the local waters. Thus was the beginning of a friendship that has lasted well over 30 years. His patience with my questions, and his love of manatees, instilled in me an appreciation for and curiosity about nature that started me down the path as a scientist, following and studying sea cows in some of the most remote areas of Africa, the Caribbean, South and Central America and Australia.

Growing up in Florida, with manatees in my 'backyard', gave me a deep affection for their gentle nature, primitive beauty and their innate curiosity about their aquatic world. One of the most curious things about manatees and one that continues to intrigue me to this day, is how can these placid creatures that suffer so at the hands of man and his machines, approach and actively solicit human contact: not to be fed or rewarded in any other way but to be touched. No matter how badly these animals may be tormented, I have never seen antagonistic behavior toward people in over 30 years of

Manatees can be difficult to see since they tend to live in turbid water and surface to breathe with just the tip of their snout showing above the water. Their stealth is critical since manatees are still hunted throughout most of their range.

observations. Only once did I even get a glimpse of what could come close to aggression, when a mother wedged herself between me and her calf when I accidentally got a bit too close to her baby.

Sea cows have played a very important role in our own mythology. The popular tales of mermaids emerged from the imagination of sailors after they mistook them for maidens. Their order, Sirenia, is derived from this close association with sirens of the sea or mermaids. Practically everywhere sea cows are found, local people link them with myths and stories usually associated with woman, reproduction, lost lovers, availability of food, pregnancy or children.

It is believed that all the sirenian populations have declined in historical times because of hunting and changes in habitat. In some areas of the world their numbers have been completely extirpated. Even though sirenians are protected in every country where they are found, hunting persists due to lack of enforcement and political will. Dugong and manatee meat can still be found in local markets around the world. In Florida, and elsewhere such as Belize, manatee deaths attributed to collisions with motorboats are rising. It now comprises over 25 per cent of the known causes for manatee mortality in Florida. Entanglement in nets and fishing gear is a problem for manatees and the main cause of deaths of dugongs, which are frequently caught in shark and turtle nets. Dugongs are also vulnerable to oil spills, storms and dynamite fishing.

Much of what we know today about manatees was first described by Hartman from his work in Crystal River. Many of our most recent findings, using satellite tracking and other types of technology, have simply provided the evidence to support his earlier observations and speculations. Much of our research today has focused on obtaining a higher level of resolution or 'fine tuning' information needed by managers to implement strategic conservation measures. For example, managers are less likely to ask the question of manatee biologists, 'Where do manatees go?', as was the case during Hartman's study, compared to asking, 'How much time do manatees spend in boat channels compared to outside marked boat channels?' The reason is so that conservation measures can be directed exactly where they are most needed, toward slowing boats to reduce manatee/boat collisions. Needless to mention, this is a difficult task and the demands are great on the biologist to provide this level of detail.

Origins

Like the more familiar whales, dolphins (cetaceans), walruses, sea lions and seals (pinnipeds), manatees and dugongs are marine mammals. Even though they share many of the same characteristics, such as body shape, flippers, smooth skin, and nostrils that close, they are not related to other marine mammals. Scientists once believed manatees were a tropical form of a walrus, since their head and muzzle look quite similar. Manatees and dugongs, collectively called sirenians or sea cows, are actually in the order Sirenia (named after sirens of Homeric origin). They belong to an interesting group of mammals referred to as subungulates and may be distantly related to ungulates or hooved mammals such as cattle, horses and deer. The subungulates include three other seemingly quite divergent mammalian orders: the elephants (Proboscidea), hyraxes (order Hyracoidea), and aardvarks (order Tubulidentata). They share certain anatomical characteristics, such as the presence of nails or hooves, and lack a clavicle. Genetic studies support this evolutional relationship and common ancestry.

Of the once diverse group of sirenians, only four species remain today: a single species of dugong and three species of manatees. The Stellar's sea cow, which was a dugongid, existed until just over 200 years ago, when it was hunted to extinction by man rather than succumbing to long-term global environmental changes that led to the demise of its relatives.

Within the order Sirenia, there are just two families, the dugongs (Dugongidae) containing only one extant species called the dugong (*Dugong dugon*) and the manatees (Trichechidae), of which there are three species: the West Indian manatee (*Trichechus manatus*), the West African manatee (*Trichechus senegalensis*) and the Amazonian manatee (*Trichechus innuguis*). The West Indian manatee has two subspecies. One, known as the Florida manatee (*Trichechus manatus latirostris*), is found in Florida and occasionally ventures as far north as Connecticut and possibly west along the Gulf of Mexico to Texas. Waifs are also known to reach the Bahamas. The other, called the Antillean manatee (*Trichechus manatus*

Manatees were once thought to be a cousin to walruses, because of their facial resemblance.

manatus), ranges along the coasts of Central and South America and may reach as far south as Recife. They are also found in the Greater Antilles, including Cuba, Jamaica, Hispaniola and Puerto Rico, with ephemeral stragglers to the smaller islands. The etymological origin of the genus *Trichechus* refers to the sparse hairs found all over the body of manatees.

The dugong (*Dugong dugon*), which is found in the Indo-Pacific region, is the only surviving member of a once diverse family of dugongids.

Like other mammals, sirenians breathe air, give birth to live young, produce milk and have hair. They closely resemble the whales and dolphins, a result of adaptation for an aquatic life. To survive, they must be agile in the water, possess specialized appendages for swimming, morphological adaptations to regulate heat, nostrils that close to block out water and have a streamlined body shape to reduce hydrodynamic drag. Sirenians still possess vestigial remnants of their ancestral terrestrial life such as finger bones and pelvic structures.

So how did sirenians evolve? Dr. Daryl Domning of Howard University has spent his life asking this question and he has contributed greatly to our understanding of sirenian evolution. It is believed that sirenians first appeared about 55 to 50 million years ago during the Eocene epoch. The earliest fossils are from Jamaica, called *Prorastomus sirenoides*, but most paleontologists think that they originated in Africa or Eurasia. A truly intermediate form was recently discovered in Jamaica and also dates from the Eocene, called *Pezosiren portelli*. This semi-aquatic creature was a little less than 3 ft (1m) high, stood on four legs and had heavy bones, typical of sirenians. Sirenians appeared to flourish during the Oligocene and Miocene Epochs around 35 to 10 million years ago. Most were dugong-like animals and were found in coastal areas around the world. Dugongid remains dating back to the Eocene have been recovered in marine fossil deposits from Europe, the southeastern United States, the Caribbean, South America, the North Pacific and Indian Ocean. One line and seemingly most common early dugongid was the genus *Metaxytherium*, which is thought to be the ancestor of our living dugong and the recently extirpated Stellar's sea cow. *Metaxytherium* is known to have passed from the Atlantic to the Pacific through the central American divide that once existed. Interestingly, dugong fossils are not uncommon

Dugongs are well adapted to the open conditions of their marine environment (above). They are relatively strong swimmers with a streamlined shape and a fluked tail like a dolphin.

Manatees inhabit inshore areas and riverine habitats (right). They have a large paddle-shaped tail looking much like an enormous beaver's. Manatees use their tails to swim with broad up and down strokes, but they can perform slow-motion barrel rolls, banking turns and spirals by curling, twisting and folding the margins of their tails.

Manatees have large, muscular lip pads that are highly movable and prehensile. They can move and manipulate their lip pads with such dexterity, aided by the hundreds of stiff bristles covering the muzzle, that they can break off the tough stems and leaves of reedy bank grasses or delicately pick up small leafy tidbits of food from the bottom.

in Florida and can be found far inland in phosphate excavations, lodged in sediments remaining from when the peninsula was once covered by the sea.

The ancestral epicenter for manatees, according to Dr. Domning, is South America. Early descendents of sirenians reached what is today South America probably during the Eocene and became isolated from other sirenians forms in their inland habitat and evolved into a distinct ancestral line that later became the manatees. The earliest known manatee fossil, Potamosiren, dating back to the middle Miocene, originated in Columbia. This early manatee-like animal lived about 15 million years ago and was recognizable as a sirenian, but had not yet evolved special dental adaptations for feeding on an abrasive diet of aquatic grasses. It seems that these early manatees or trichechids inhabited coastal estuaries and rivers, a more freshwater existence than the dugongs, which typically were found in more marine environments. Manatees tended to feed on freshwater vegetation, whereas dugongids grazed on seagrasses. During the late Miocene, manatees became isolated in the Amazon basin when geological events led to the emergence of the Andes mountains and the closure of the Pacific entrance to the Amazon River that had previously existed. Erosion of the newly emerged Andes greatly increased the amount of sediments and nutrients released into the Amazonian aquatic system. By the late Miocene and early Pliocene, aquatic grasses and vegetation proliferated but their leaf and stems contained high levels of silica and also tended to trap sediments. This food source for manatees was nutritious, but highly abrasive. To cope with this abrasive diet, manatees evolved specialized teeth. One ancestral line of manatees remained in the Amazon basin subsisting on overhanging and floating vegetation and became the Amazonian manatee. Another group emerged from the Amazon into the Caribbean.

In the Indian and Pacific Oceans, dugongids also evolved a unique dental mechanism to compensate for increasing siltation in their marine habitats caused by glaciation. By the Pliocene, dugongs had evolved an alternative way to deal with tooth abrasion caused by their seagrass diet. Instead of replacing teeth, dugongs have molars that continually grow upward as they are worn down. Dugongids in the Caribbean, however, failed to evolve effective tooth replacement, and as seagrasses became heavily silted during the highly erosional periods; during glaciation episodes when sea levels dropped, erosion and sedimentation increased and coastal shelves became limited, these New World dugongs could not survive. Manatees, on the other hand, according to Domning, could cope with the highly abrasive diet and those that made it to the Caribbean replaced the dugongs, becoming the West Indian manatee (*Trichechus manatus*). A common ancestor eventually made its way to West Africa to emerge as the third manatee, now known as the West African manatee (*Trichechus senegalensis*).

The Steller's sea cow (*Hydrodamalis gigas*) was probably one of the most unusual sea cows. It was large – at least 26 ft (8 m) long – and probably weighed between 4 and 10 metric tons. We don't know the exact weight since no weights were known to be recorded. This creature, unlike the other sirenians, was not found in warmer tropical waters but rather capitalized on abundant algae in the colder waters of the northern Pacific. The Steller's sea cow had no teeth and used a hard, bony palate to macerate its diet of algae. They also lacked finger bones and had club-like appendages for foreflippers that they used to grasp rocky outcroppings and stabilize themselves in the ocean swell as they fed. Our knowledge about the Steller's sea cow's origins is incomplete. Domning has described how, during the Miocene epoch, dugongids derived from *Metaxytherium* began to spread northward along the Pacific coast of North America. One of these early sea cow forms, *Dusisiren jordani*, lived about 10 to 12 million years ago along the coast of California. It was larger than most sirenians and, unlike other dugongs, did not have tusks. Another primitive sea cow, *Dusisiren dewana*, lived about 9 million years ago on the opposite side of the Pacific along the coast of Japan. This species had modified finger and wrist bones and a reduction of its teeth. It probably represented an intermediate stage between other dugongids and the Steller's sea cow. About three to eight million years ago a creature very similar to the Steller's, called *Hydrodamalis cuestae*, inhabited the eastern Pacific. This sea cow was large, perhaps bigger than Steller's sea cow, and also lacked teeth. It is estimated from fossil skull fragments that this sirenian giant probably grew to a length of over 30 feet (9 m).

A dugong avoids the photographer by using its pectoral fins to turn quickly. All of the sirenians use their flippers extensively not only for swimming but also to clasp each other and to aid with manipulating food.

Form and Function

The day I arrived in West Africa to begin a three-year study of manatees in Ivory Coast, a local biologist told me that he had never seen wild manatees after years of searching and that I would be lucky to see one, let alone capture and radio-tag some! Fortunately, the next week, knowing where to look and by flying aerial surveys, I saw my first West African manatees in the Bandama River. But he was correct, I was very lucky, because what I discovered over the course of my research, was that manatees are extremely secretive and difficult to see, though there may be quite a few around. This is an adaptive behavioral trait, since manatees were heavily hunted.

Because of their secretive habits, it is often difficult to get good information about their biology. Much of what we first learned about manatees and dugongs was from fishermen or hunters, because to be good at catching them you must know their habits very well. In many instances, however, what we were told by fishermen, like fishermen's tales everywhere, was exaggerated, wrong or steeped in local mythology.

Sirenians are now among the best-studied marine mammals in the world. Albeit, there are still certain aspects about their biology that remains unknown, and we sometimes need higher resolution of information to improve and strategically plan conservation actions. We know that sea cows are well adapted to their completely aquatic life. They are streamlined with torpedo-shaped bodies, no dorsal fin, no hind-limbs, a few sparse hairs and forelimbs called flippers that are semi-movable and paddle-shaped. They use their flippers to maneuver by sculling, rotating or paddling. Sea cows have two nostrils located at the tip of their muzzle, rather than a blowhole situated on the back of their head like a cetacean. The nostrils can be closed with a flap of skin to prevent water from entering when they submerge.

Watching manatees and dugongs in the water is like observing a slow underwater ballet. Sometimes they appear to float effortlessly through the water, rising and sinking at will and seemingly without motion of their flippers. This remarkable ability to control their buoyancy is achieved by compressing and shifting the distribution of air in their lungs with their long diaphragm. Ballast is created by their dense, heavy bones (referred to as pachyostotic bones) and, surprisingly, by the weight of their skin which equals 70 per cent of the negative buoyant force of their heavy bones. There is a lingering question as to how manatees can so easily remain neutrally buoyant as they move between salt- and freshwater, as saltwater is denser than freshwater, so they should float or sink to the bottom in freshwater!

Manatees and dugongs feed on a wide variety of seagrasses and freshwater aquatic vegetation. Manatees can sometimes be seen feeding on vegetation overhanging the water or fruits and nuts that have fallen into the water. I have been surprised to see a manatee with its body halfway out of the water feeding on bank grass or clipping lawn grass at the water's edge. They will eat practically any vegetable matter in contact with the water and will occasionally ingest a variety of trash items such as discarded fishing line, plastic bags, rope, small toy balls – practically anything they can swallow. Sometimes these items get stuck in their gut or, in the case of fish hooks, can puncture their intestinal or stomach lining, leading to death by secondary infection. Manatees at least, are not strict herbivores; in Jamaica, I observed West Indian manatees stealing fish out of nets.

Sirenians use their thick, movable lip pads to grasp and move vegetation toward their mouth. They have a marvelous mechanism for transporting the food with their movable lip pads. On the underside of the muzzle, the lips have several rows of stiff bristles or hairs called vibrissae. Each vibrissa resides in a small cavity with only the tip of the bristle exposed above the skin. While eating they can extend and retract these specialized whiskers so they act somewhat like the legs of a centipede marching and guiding the bits of food toward their mouth. The tongue then takes over and maneuvers the food to the teeth for mastication. From time to time, I've let a manatee grasp my hand in its lip pads and mouth. Its hundreds of little bristles and moving lip pads feel like some sort of bizarre industrial brush machine vacuuming and scrubbing my hand. Only when my hand and arm have disappeared up to my elbow have I pulled free, and with quite some effort, for fear of the molars making painful contact with my fingers.

Seagrasses and other aquatic plants have leaves or stems that can contain high proportions of silica and minerals. These aquatic plants are frequently encrusted with various organisms, called epiphytes, calcium deposits, sand or silt. To compensate for the abrasive effects of their herbivorous diet, sirenians have evolved two novel mechanisms for replacing worn teeth. Dugongs possess three pairs of molars and three

A manatee has pulled a water hyacinth underwater and holds it with its flippers so it can feed on the leaves and petioles. After clipping off the upper part of the plant, the manatee lets the remains float back to the surface. When studying manatees we sometimes can follow a trail of topless water hyacinths back to where they are feeding.

A pair of manatees surface in one of Florida's clear freshwater springs.

pairs of premolars in each jaw. As the individual grows older, the first set of molars and all of the premolars are lost. The two sets of molars that remain in each jaw continue to grow upward for the life of the dugong, something like a 'push-up' popsicle. In addition to the complement of molars, male, and very rarely female, dugongs have two large incisors that erupt through the gums called tusks (harking back to their shared lineage with elephants), which can be seen only when the mouth is open. The tusks appear to be used primarily during reproductive activities rather than to aid in feeding. Some of the dugong's ancestors, however, did seem to use their tusks to cut or excavate rhizomes.

Manatees have evolved another method for dealing with tooth wear. Unlike dugongs, which replace their teeth by growing them longer as they wear down, manatees create new teeth. As the animal ages the molars migrate forward in the jaw. The oldest teeth and those closest to the front have their roots absorbed. Eventually these older and worn teeth fall out. In fact, it is sometimes possible to reach into the mouth of a live manatee and pluck out a tooth at the front of the jaw with your fingers that was just about ready to fall out anyway. While the worn teeth are falling out in the front of the jaw, new ones are being formed and emerge at the back of the jaw. So the process continues through the animal's life, like a conveyor belt, with new teeth coming in from the back, slowly moving forward to replace the older, worn ones that have fallen out in the front.

Sirenians have no external genitalia. Males have a genital aperture situated about halfway down the belly and females have an opening near the anus close to the tail stock called the caudal peduncle. There are no external ears on either manatees or dugongs and the auditory opening is a small pinhole that is very difficult to see. The small opening is located behind the eye about the same distance as that between the eye and the tip of the muzzle.

Senses

Sirenians have all the senses we know as humans, including sight, touch, taste, smell and hearing. Since they live underwater some senses are better adapted to their aquatic environment than our own. Because they frequently live in turbid water, they do not utilize their eyesight to the extent that we do. Their eye contains both rods and cones, suggesting that they see colors and can function in dim light. Recent investigations at Mote Marine Laboratory on captive manatees have shown that manatees do not have exceedingly good visual acuity, i.e. they could be considered to be legally blind! Personally, I have observed manatees turn and look at me from about 30 to 40 feet (9 to 12m) away and then swim directly toward me, which would lead me to believe that they saw me from that distance.

Their hearing is similar to other marine mammals and they can detect underwater sounds from a

Radio-tagging helps researchers.

hundred or more meters. Hunters in Africa know well that the slightest sound, such as a paddle bumping the side of a canoe, can send a manatee fleeing. Manatees have large earbones suggesting that they have a keen sense of hearing. Vocalizations between a mother and calf enable the pair to stay in contact and locate each other in turbid water. On one occasion in Belize, when we were capturing manatees to radio-tag them, a mother and her calf were encircled in the net. I was helping to direct capture operations by making observations from a hovering helicopter. The mother quickly escaped from the net and swam about half a mile away. As soon as her calf was released from the net, the mother turned completely around and made a direct track for her calf. The calf, as well, headed straight for its mother. When the two met, they swam off together. At that distance it would have been impossible for the two to see each other and though we did not have a hydrophone in the water, it's almost certain that they heard each other vocalizing and were able to locate and orient toward the sounds they emitted. They do not seem to hear above-surface sounds unless they are exceedingly loud. Some studies suggest that manatees hear higher frequency sounds better than lower frequencies. Boating advocates have interpreted this to mean that manatees do not hear slower boats that emit lower frequency sounds than fast moving watercraft. Observations of wild manatees do not support this contention since manatees react to slowly moving boats from distances of half a mile or more. Though they may hear higher-frequency sounds better, they have a wide range of hearing that includes lower-frequency sounds such as slowly moving boats.

Little is known about their senses of taste and smell. Manatees have taste buds and anatomical adaptations that suggest they may be able to smell. They have distinct food preferences and will sometimes mouth or chew new foods before swallowing or rejecting them, probably using taste to recognize familiar foods. Manatees will frequently chew novel items such as plastic rope and other trash found in the water, suggesting that taste is an important sensory factor. When individuals meet they tend to sweep their mouths over each other, perhaps picking up particular tastes that aid in individual recognition. Chemoreception may also enable males to locate and distinguish estrous females. The fact that manatees can navigate through labyrinthine waterways where the water is opaque would suggest that they may use chemoreceptive capabilities to distinguish the unique chemical signatures of specific waterways. Hearing may also play a similar role since the aquatic environment contains many sounds.

Manatees are tactile animals and tame individuals will seek out rubbing and stroking from divers. They also will rub on rocks or logs lying on the bottom. They have even been known to scratch on the propellers of outboard motors (not running). Mothers and calves maintain very close physical contact. New studies by researchers at the University of Florida have shown that manatees use the sparse, evenly spaced hairs scattered all over their backs to detect slight vibrations in the water. These hairs may be sensitive receptors akin to the lateral line of a fish.

Dugongs have smooth skin that can range in color from brownish to gray. The skin is covered with sparse hairs. Manatees tend to have rougher skin, with the exception of the Amazonian manatee which has smooth skin and white to pinkish patches on its ventral side. This species also is blackish in color compared to the other two species of manatees that are generally brown to gray, depending on whether their backs are covered with fresh - or saltwater algae.

At birth, dugongs are about 3 ft 6 in (1.15 m) long and weigh around 60 to 70 lb (25 to 35 kg). West Indian manatees are known to range from 2 ft 6 in to 5 ft 2 in (80 to 160 cm) but typically are around 3 ft (100 cm). They usually weigh around 66 lb (30 kg) when born. Little is known about the size at birth of the West African manatee but based on what is known, they are similar in size to the West

Indian species. Amazonian manatees are smaller, they measure about 2 ft 6 in to 2 ft 9 in (75 to 85 cm) and weigh between 22 and 33 lb (10 to 15 kg) when born.

Adult dugongs can reach 13 ft (4.1 m) long but typically are about 11 ft (3.3 m) in length. They can weigh up to 2200 lb (1000 kg) and the maximum recorded age, based on growth rings in the tusk, is 73 years. The largest recorded West Indian manatee was a female that had reached a length of 13 ft (4.1 m) and the largest male was 12 ft (3.7 m) long. The heaviest manatee recorded was an 11 ft long (3.4 m) female whose carcass weighed 3564 lb (1620 kg). Females typically are larger than males. The oldest known West Indian manatee, based on counting annual growth bands in the earbones, lived to be 59 years, when it was killed by a motorboat. A captive manatee named Snooty has lived for over 54 years, which suggests that manatees can live to 60 or 70 years old. The maximum recorded measurements for the West African manatees are 9 ft 10 in (3 m) for a female and 10 ft 10 in (3.3 m) for a male, and they probably can weigh over 2200 lb (1000 kg), but far fewer West African manatees have been caught and measured compared to the other two species. Amazonian manatees are smaller and the longest one of this species was 9 ft (2.8 m) long and weighed about 1100 lb (500 kg). Their lifespan is unknown but probably similar to dugongs and West Indian manatees.

Manatees are very efficient herbivores. They extract much of the nutritional and caloric value from their food before it passes out of the digestive system. Sirenians are hindgut digesters like horses and elephants. Several byproducts are created during digestion including copious amounts of methane gas.

Most marine mammals live strictly in saltwater and cannot thrive in freshwater, due to osmotic imbalances. Dugongs are found only in marine habitats. The Amazonian manatee is restricted to the freshwater Amazon Basin and may occasionally descend into brackish water. By contrast, the West Indian and the West African manatees can move freely between saltwater and freshwater habitats. Both species appear to be attracted to sources of freshwater. In Florida, West Indian manatees can often be seen drinking freshwater emanating from storm drains or even gulping water from running hoses dangling from a dock. In West Africa this attraction to freshwater can be hazardous, since manatee hunters sometimes build platforms next to freshwater springs that are situated in salt or brackish water habitats. The hunters place a ring of small sticks in the muddy bottom around the spring and wait on the platform at night. When the manatees come to the spring to drink, they squeeze through the sticks, making them move and separate, thus alerting the hunter, who quietly readies himself on the platform over the spring and then harpoons the manatee once it has settled in to drink.

John Reynolds, who has studied manatee physiology and behavior for many years, and others have suggested that the manatee kidney structure can allow it to concentrate its urine, minimizing loss of freshwater. Manatees, like other marine mammals, may also metabolize fat reserves to internally produce freshwater. We do know that they live in areas where there is little freshwater available, but tend to be more abundant in regions where the water is brackish or fresh; or, if found in marine habitats, where there is a source of freshwater such as a river, streams, offshore springs or even sewage outfalls. Amazonian manatees live entirely in freshwater so do not have to contend with the osmotic difficulties as the other two species of manatees.

Sirenians, like other marine mammals, need to hold their breath for a long time. A large manatee can stay below the surface for up to 20 minutes. Personally, I have recorded a sleeping manatee staying submerged for over 16 minutes. More typically they tend to stay submerged for around two to three minutes, but longer when resting or more frequently when they are active. Studies show that they may slow their heartbeats when submerging or if they need to stay submerged. For example, Amazonian manatees are known to slow their heart rate from 40 beats a minute to eight beats when they are frightened. When sirenians breathe they usually surface with just the tip of their two nostrils showing above the surface. If swimming they may make a rolling dive like a cetacean. Humans usually exchange about 10 per cent of their lung capacity when taking a breath while resting. Sirenians are much more efficient and renew about 90 per cent of the air in their lungs with each breath. The lungs of a manatee are flat and about 3 feet 6 inches (1 m) long, with major bronchi or airways that extend practically the entire length. What's unusual is that each lung has its own diaphragm, called hemidiaphragms, and if one lung or diaphragm is damaged, say by a boat strike, this peculiar anatomy may allow each lung to act semi-independently.

Manatees and dugongs are primarily found in the warmer tropical coastal and inland waters of the world. The Florida subspecies of the West Indian manatee, however, is at the climatic extreme of its range, where each winter it encounters more temperate waters and where air temperatures can drop below freezing. Dugongs in Australia also reach lower latitudes where climatic conditions are more temperate. Florida manatees in the southeastern United States and dugongs in Australia move each year in response to cooler winter temperatures. Researchers in Australia have noticed northward movements each winter of dugongs in Shark Bay in western Australia and in Moreton Bay in eastern Australia to escape cooler water and air temperatures.

In Florida, each winter, manatees aggregate in spring-fed headwaters of several rivers and streams where the water temperatures rarely drop below 72°F (22.2°C). This adaptable species has also taken advantage of the warm water emanating from industrial power plants. These movements have been well documented through radio and satellite telemetry. In general, as seasonal temperatures begin to drop in the autumn manatees begin to move southward from the northern extremities of their range, which in rare instances can reach as far north as Connecticut on the east coast of the United States, and to the northwest and west at least to Louisiana on the Gulf of Mexico coast. Once the manatees return to Florida they either continue to the southern region of the State or they move into the relatively tepid headwaters of spring-fed rivers and the discharge waters of power plants. Some of these areas, both natural and artificial, can harbor over 300 manatees during extremely cold weather. The manatees don't tend to stay in these warm waters throughout the winter. Typically they converge on these warm water refugia soon after or during the passage of a cold frontal weather system. During the day, the animals may venture out into cooler water to feed, returning later to the warmth of the sanctuary. Between the passages of these cold frontal systems, air temperatures can moderate quickly and many manatees may move between warm water refugia or make excursions quite far from the warm water sanctuaries only to return when temperatures drop again.

Each winter some manatees succumb to the cold weather and die due to a cold-stress syndrome that is characterized by loss of fat, white pigmentation akin to frost bite on the extremities, ulcerations on the skin and impacted intestines. This cold stress-related mortality can be a slow, chronic condition that becomes complicated by opportunistic infections, which can occur when the animals are exposed to cold water for extended periods such as occurred in Florida during the winter of 2000-2001. That particular winter most of the cold-related deaths occurred in the southern portion where normally they would be safe from the cold, but where there are few power plants and springs for refuge. In more northern areas of Florida, even though temperatures were lower, the situation was different. Where manatees had sought sanctuary in power plants and springs, they fared much better and survived, probably because they could stay warm through most of the day in the warm water and were only exposed to the coldest temperatures when they had to venture out to feed. When satiated or cold they could return to the warmth of the spring or effluent.

Manatees can also die relatively quickly from a hypothermic condition after just a few hours of exposure to cold water. This can occur when a manatee is caught far from a source of warm water during an extreme cold period and a rapid drop in temperature. One such situation occurred in 1977 when a power plant in Brevard County shut down during the height of severe cold, exposing over 100 manatees to low temperatures. During a two-week period 38 manatee carcasses were recovered from the area.

Manatees do not possess true blubber, instead they have thickened skin and a fat layer that provides poor insulation against cold. They are a tropical animal, adapted for 'dumping' excess heat rather than conserving it. Their metabolic rate is lower than a mammal of similar size and they only have a limited ability to increase their metabolism to produce additional heat. Manatees also seem to 'shut-down' when they are very cold, that is they stop moving around and cease feeding, to conserve their remaining heat. Younger animals, weaned from their mothers, seem to be the most vulnerable to cold-related stress and

mortality. Their relatively large surface area to body mass ratio contributes to their difficulty in regulating body heat. They may also lack the knowledge about where to go to stay warm if caught by cold weather away from their usual winter warm water refuge. Dependent calves, since they are still nursing, obtain warmth and a high-quality food from their mother's milk. They also benefit from being with their mother who probably was quick to find warmer water.

Reproduction

Female West Indian manatees can begin reproducing at about 3½ years old and probably continue to have young until late in life. We know little about the reproductive biology for the other two species of manatees, so we assume that they have similar reproductive habits.

When in estrus a female manatee attracts a mating herd of males. These highly active mating herds may remain with the female for more than two weeks and can number 20 or more males. The composition of the herd is dynamic and not all the males will remain with the female the entire time. These mating herds are constantly moving as the females tries to elude her suitors. The males swarm over and under her, jostling to gain a position close and advantageous for the moment she is receptive to mating. Consequently, there is constant and vigorous bumping, rolling, pushing and positioning by the males.

On several occasions I have been caught in the middle of this mating mêlée when I tried to insert myself into the middle of the herd in order to glimpse and identify the estrus female and her suitors. It goes without saying, one does not quickly forget being jostled and surrounded by 20 tons of sex-driven sirenians. The female, after weeks of harassment, will sometimes beach herself to thwart her pursuers' attempts to get underneath her and to have some respite from their constant attentions.

Individuals, both males and females and with partners of either sex, engage in sex play. They often grasp each other with flippers, mouthing genitals, rolling and cavorting. Gestation is between 12 and 14 months and usually a single calf is born, but twins represent a little less than 2 per cent of the births. Calves remain with the mother until they wean, which can vary from a year to about 18 months. It nurses by grasping the upper part of the mother's flipper in its mouth and sucking from the teat located at the base and rear of her flipper. Some anecdotal information and opportunistic observations by manatee biologists suggest that female manatees may occasionally leave their calves unattended in quiet, sheltered areas for hours at a time while they go off to feed, returning a few hours later to fetch their offspring. Mating and calving can occur at any time of the year, but in Florida calving and breeding may peak in the spring when the energetic demands of winter are finished. This reproductive strategy helps the female through the energetic stress of pregnancy or nursing when there is abundant food and warm water during the summer. Amazonian manatees may also time their breeding and calving to synchronize with the rainy season when resources are more available. In Africa, where there are severe dry seasons, I noted and was told by fishermen that there is a peak calving and breeding season just before the rains begin. On average, females have calves about every 2½ years.

Dugongs appear to have a similar mating system to manatees with one exception, in Shark Bay, Australia. Here, males appear to establish territories where they display by making rushing passes to attract females. Elsewhere a female in estrus attracts a herd of males similar to manatees. The dugong mating process has several phases, including a 'following phase' characterized by the males forming a cohesive group around the female as she swims and tries to avoid their attentions. This phase is followed by intense activities as the males lunge, twist, tail-slap and thrash around the female. Finally this heightened activity transforms into a 'mounting phase' in which a male clasps the female from below while others hold on with their flippers around other parts of her body. Gestation is between 12 to 14 months and calves are weaned around 18 months. Calves can remain with their mothers for several years, however. Calving intervals can range from 2½ to 7 years and can occur at any time of the year in tropical regions, whereas in more temperate areas there appears to be a seasonal peak.

Feeding

Manatees feed on a wide selection of aquatic and semi-aquatic plants, including marine and freshwater. They have been observed feeding on bank growth and even lawn grass growing next to the water's edge. In West Africa, fishermen have told me about seeing branches of mangrove, a tree that grows in and along the water's edge in estuaries and river mouths, fly out of the water as the fisherman paddles past. Apparently the manatee will reach up and grab a mangrove branch with its mouth and then pull it down and hold it under the water while grasping it with their flippers. They hold it like this munching on the leaves until startled by the passing pirogue and then let go of the branch sending it flying back out of the water – sometimes upsetting the fisherman's canoe. Both manatees and dugongs have large, massive muzzles that are capable of grasping and uprooting vegetation. When feeding on stiff bank grasses in West Africa, they grab the stem of the plant and twist it until it breaks off at a node, leaving a very characteristic trail of twisted stems and leaves along the water's edge.

Social Structure

Even though they can form large aggregations, for example at warm water sites, most frequently they are sighted alone or in small ephemeral groups. Manatees are attracted to fresh water, abundant sources of food, good resting areas and places where there is minimal human disturbance; consequently you may find manatees at higher densities around these shared resources. The strongest social bond is between a mother and its calf. Usually the pair stay in close contact with each other and frequently vocalize back and forth using high-pitched squeaks and squeals. If threatened or startled the calf may let out a squeal that initiates a rapid duet of squeaks between the cow and calf. Males sometimes accompany females or females with calves for days at a time, probably in anticipation of the female entering estrus. There are no family units of mother, father and calf.

Dugongs seem to be a more social species compared to manatees. They tend to form small groups of up to six individuals, but larger groups have been seen. It's not known why the animals form these larger aggregations. Like the manatees, the strongest social bond is between the cow and calf.

A Year in the Life of a Florida Manatee

The following chapter is a fictitious account of a year in the life of a manatee that lives in Northwest Florida. This the area where I grew up and have studied manatees for over 30 years. The story incorporates much of what we know about the biology of manatees and includes many actual observations. I have also taken literary license to include some speculative insights into manatee behavior and abilities. What is told here is based on what is already known, current hypotheses and on-going research.

She can taste the trail of sweetness in the water as she glides through the darkness with the gentle, slow strokes of her tail. She knows exactly where she is even though the water is dark this time of night. The water around Cedar Keys on the northwest gulf coast of Florida is rich in phytoplankton and nearly opaque. As she swims through the labyrinthine channels created by the numerous oyster beds, she listens for the unique sounds of each one and the distinctive taste of the water. Each channel is slightly different from the next with its own peculiar complement of sounds from snapping shrimp, grunts and the noise of lapping waves over the oyster bars. It's an acoustically rich environment. Usually it is dominated by the loud drone of numerous outboard engines, but late at night, she only hears the twang of a single, far off outboard. Probably a commercial crabber getting an early start checking his stone crab traps. Her back is scarred from the blows and lacerations from at least 20 previous hits from the skegs, drive shafts or propellers of motorboats, one set for each year of her life. Biologists have entered her image into a computer photographic identification catalogue that contains close to a thousand individually recognizable manatees. Each animal is catalogued by its unique complement of scars. One of the biologists that first photographed her gave her the name 'Tia'.

What pushes Tia on, however, is a slight sweet taste of freshwater, spiced with a trace of her preferred food from her favorite feeding ground. She recalls the foraging site well and follows the trail of 'scents' she encounters, the distinctive noises and the occasional visual landmark of a log or rock on the bottom. Her ultimate destination is a shoal near the mouth of the East Pass of the Suwannee River. The water has a unique chemical signature created by merging and mixing of waters from the Suwannee and several other creeks. Tia was brought to this particular place 20 years ago by her mother and she has returned every year since she was born. She learned the route from her mother while accompanying her when she was a calf. If you're a manatee or an elephant, its relative, an excellent memory is important to remember the location of distant feeding grounds or alternative sources of warm water, particularly if one year your favorite one disappears. Some manatees may travel many hundreds of kilometers during the course of their annual migration and wanderings.

This year she's pregnant and near term, so it is more important for her to find East Pass since this area is rich with her favorite and nutritious food, shoal grass, which grows where the water is brackish, not too salty. This is good since she will not have to contend with ridding herself of so much excess salt from the water she may ingest while feeding. The leaves of shoal grass are thin and stringy, not much plant in a single mouthful compared to lush turtle grass or manatee grass that lives in full salt water. Shoal grass leaves are also relatively clean without the carpet of epiphytes, organisms that grow on the blade and can sometimes contain toxins, or heavy with calcium deposits that form on the blades of turtle and manatee grass.

As she nears her destination, there is the distinctive sound of other manatees munching away at this lush bed of shoal grass. The feeding manatees sound something like walking on crusty snow, 'crunch', 'crunch', 'crunch', with each chew. Every minute or so, the crunching stops and she hears the tearing of the leaf blades from their roots as a manatee wraps its massive lips around a bunch of leaves. It holds the plant firmly with hundreds of bristles on its lips, which are intertwined with the mass of leaves and rhizomes, and pulls the plant free from the bottom.

She arrives at East Pass as the sun rises and the surface mist begins to be swept away by the morning breeze. The water is ripe with familiar tastes or 'scents', particularly those of individual manatees. She can tell who's there from the lingering scents coming from the manatee dung on the bottom and from minute traces in the water of urine laced with hormones. This cocktail of tastes probably tells her the sex of nearby individuals and the reproduction condition of the females. She goes straight toward a particular female whose individual scent trail is recognizable and familiar. The signature scent is from her calf of the previous season. For a year and a half this little female had been her constant companion. Now she is here alone, having returned to this rich patch of food where she had been led by her mother for two seasons. The mother collides with her offspring with a gentle, brushing roll. Tia lightly grazes her lips across her daughter's back, and takes in the familiar taste. They surface together with their muzzles touching and exchange a few squeaks of recognition, then feed adjacent to each other, occasionally squeaking to acknowledge that they are together. Tia is hungry after a day of swimming with little or no food. Over the next day, she consumes about 155 lb (70 kg) of aquatic vegetation, around 10 per cent of her body weight.

This year Tia has no calf, but she is plump and round with a near-term fetus. She looks like a caricature of a manatee with a swollen and blimpish body. About a year before, and not long after she had successfully slipped away from her 18-month-old calf, she entered estrus. She knew well what this would entail, her scent, ripe with hormones, followed her everywhere she swam. Like heat-seeking missiles, male manatees began to converge on her. The herd of sex-driven males constantly clambered over and under her. She could rarely sleep during this time and could only occasionally pause to feed. The squeaks and squeals of the swirling mass of bodies were nearly constant as they bumped and bounced off each other. There was no peace. She finally found some rest by beaching herself on a soft sand bar for an entire day. The water was shallow and she rested with her back awash and burning in the sun. Using their pectoral fins, the males crawled into the shallow water, trying to reach her. They could climb over and around her, but not underneath where they could probe her genital region. Several times during the end of the two weeks she felt the urge to succumb and mated with some of the largest males who had the stamina and strength to push away the others and stay close to her until she was willing.

A manatee calf suckles warm milk from her mother's teat located at the rear and base of her flipper. Calves can eat vegetation relatively soon after they are born but usually nurse for up to two years.

Within a couple of weeks after arriving at East Pass, her fetus twists and turns with more frequency. She feels the need to find the sheltered and quiet area of the bay where she has given birth before. Protected from winds and waves, with just the right conditions for birthing she feels secure. In the early morning hours, a male calf is born. This birth is easy since she is an experienced mother. The calf, just over 3 ft (1m) long, emerges tail first. The little spoon of a tail is curled around lengthwise and emerges first. The head comes last and the calf has to rise immediately for its first breath of air. He makes a couple of quick strokes with his tail and breaks free from his umbilicus and birth sack, then shoots for the surface while his mother helps by nudging him upward with her muzzle. After a few hours, her new baby easily surfaces without her assistance. He stays close, almost always touching her, for the next few days. Right now his swimming motions are jerky and exaggerated, he doesn't use his little flippers much. The slow, methodical, smooth motions will come later. He stations himself close to her head and flippers. In response to his probing, she rolls slightly and raises her flipper toward her head. The calf pokes and probes with his mouth until he finds her teat under her flipper, and latches on by holding base of her flipper in his mouth. There he happily nurses for a minute or so before having to surface to breathe. Later he will nurse for much longer periods of as long as 20 minutes.

Over the next few months the calf will grow quickly, putting on about 1 lb (500 g) a day. His mother will feed extensively to meet the energetic demands of lactation and will likely not move far from this preferred summering area at the mouth of the Suwannee River. She occasionally moves up the Suwannee in search of freshwater and may even visit Manatee Springs to feed on vegetation near its mouth. The water from Manatee Springs at 72°F (22°C) is cold compared to the river. During the winter, however, the spring water is much warmer. Even so, she won't return to Manatee Springs the following winter since her preferred winter home is in Crystal River, about 45 miles (75 km) away. Some of her ancestors, however, did use Manatee Springs to stay warm during the winter months but were extirpated about 100 years ago. Stories from the eighteenth century talk about manatee hunters using the clear, warm waters of the spring to hunt manatees, hence the name of the spring. Manatees did not regularly return to the spring until just recently.

Male manatees sometimes take up with Tia and her calf, spending several days following the pair. They pester her with sexual grasps and proddings even though she is not in estrus. She tries to avoid them and fears that her calf may be injured as the massive males maneuver around her. Some of these lone males remain in the East Pass area, while others roam far along the coast, maybe even reaching Louisiana before the end of the summer when the weather turns cooler.

In late September, the evening temperatures are beginning to drop and the water is gradually cooling from the summer highs. She knows that winter and cold weather are approaching. So even before the first cold front passes across the state, she begins meandering eastward and southward along the coast. She travels more slowly than she did the previous spring when she was headed to the Suwannee, since she has her five-month-old calf in tow. The calf is still dependent on his mother's milk, but even at this young age he starts to try the seagrasses where his mother stops to feed. By late October, the two have reached the Withlacoochee River just north of the Crystal River Nuclear Power Plant. A fast-moving cold front, the first of the year, drops the air temperature overnight to 68°F (20°C). Even before the water temperature decreases she pushes her calf to swim quickly to the power plant about 15 miles (20 km) away. In the discharge waters of the power plant, the two are joined by several other females with calves and by older manatees. The water is warm in the narrow discharge canal because it has passed through the heat exchangers of the power plant. Many of the younger manatees have stayed in the Withlacoochee not anticipating how rapidly the water temperatures in these shallow coastal areas can plunge. After a couple of days the weather clears and overnight air temperatures begin to warm. She knows that she can't stay in the canal for the winter because it is too deep and lacks food, so she decides to continue a little farther south to the headwaters of Crystal River another 10 miles (15 km) away. She passes along the shallow coast where the Gulf water has now cooled from about 80°F (27°C) three days previously to 72°F (22°C), the same temperature as the waters emanating from the artesian spring at the source of the river.

The headwaters of Crystal River are full of early arrivals, about 100 manatees; many are females with calves that have come to pass the winter in the warm water. Not until the next cold front, which will drive the Gulf water temperatures below 64°F (18°C) will the full complement of manatees arrive in the river. Several animals that are in the river are transients who will stay only a week or maybe a few days. They will wait for a warming trend and then continue to make their way further south where they will spend the winter at another source of warm water, one that's more familiar to them, probably where their mothers took them as calves to stay warm.

Once they are safely in the spring-fed river, mother and calf are relatively content in the constant 73°F (23°C) water, though it is still a bit chilly for their tropical disposition and metabolism. They arrived in the river before first light and swam directly to the main spring, called the 'boil'. The boil is bowl-shaped and about 50 ft (15 m) deep but has a cavern, which is the source of the water, that extends down to about 80 ft (25 m) below the surface. Around the edge of the spring, there are shallow limestone ledges and a sandy area that is only a few feet deep. The shallow sandy area is where they finally settle to bottom rest. They remain close together with  the calf next to its mother, his muzzle gently touching her flipper. They sleep together for the next few hours, without disturbance, regularly rising with no perceptible movements of their bodies to breathe about every six minutes. All around them are about 20 other manatees quietly sleeping on the bottom, basking in the warm water flowing over their bodies from the spring.

At dawn, they hear the unmistakable sound of an outboard motor approaching the spring. The mother becomes slightly agitated which is only noticeable by the fact that this time when she surfaces, she shifts her resting site a few feet from where she has been for the last few hours. The boat approaches closer and then stops about 55 yards (50 m) away. The people on the boat noisily heave an

Informational signs posted at boat ramps and marinas alert boaters and others to the presence of manatees, and to what rules apply to observing them or operating a boat in the area.

anchor into the water and it clanks to the bottom. Several of the manatees slowly rise and begin to idle out of the spring toward deeper water and away from the warmth of the spring boil. Mother and calf remain a little longer. A few minutes later, a horde of snorkelers are unleashed from the boat, all swimming quickly for the boil and splashing with clumsy strokes of their fins. Tia is already awake but does not move; her calf rises and turns toward the divers to watch them approaching from 30 ft (10 m) away. He has never seen such creatures or commotion before, but has no particular fear; apprehension is overcome by youthful curiosity. He moves up toward a group of divers as the other swimmers disperse around the spring watching the other manatees. Now three-quarters of the manatees have fled the spring; they left at the first sound or sight of the divers. These more skittish individuals move back out to the main channel or to a smaller nearby spring that has been cordoned off with a line of buoys to keep out snorkelers and boats. This sanctuary around the main spring was established by the U.S. Fish & Wildlife Service to provide a place for manatees to rest undisturbed near a secondary spring. During the winter, there are so many divers and so many boats, sometimes the only chance for manatees in Crystal River to have rest or feed without disturbance are in these sanctuaries where people are prevented from entering.

Two juvenile manatees resting in the spring are quite tame and approach several of the snorkelers. They roll over like dogs to have their bellies rubbed and stroked. The people are overwhelmed by the experience. They also have jumped to the conclusion, since they did not notice the other manatees leaving the spring as they entered the water, that all manatees must be this tame and friendly toward humans. In reality, the tame animals are the minority and have been unintentionally 'trained' to approach swimmers in the water by the reward of being petted. What the people do not realize is that they only get to observe this one particular unusual and unnatural behavior, albeit very exciting for them. If the people were to observe from a distance and not chase after the manatees, they might have the opportunity to observe the full spectrum of manatee behaviors including nursing, feeding, sleeping and even sexual play. Instead, they watch wild animals behave like domesticated pets.

The calf is now overcome by curiosity and ventures closer to the swimmers to get a closer look. As he does so, one of the divers spies the baby and gestures to her friends to come over. Together the divers all swim toward the calf in order to get a better look and maybe a chance to pet a 'baby manatee'. The calf stays just out of reach until one of the swimmers dives down after it just to make sure that his friend could snap a photograph. As the swimmer plunges under it, the calf lets out a loud squeal and swims rapidly to his mother, who finally has had enough. She launches herself off the bottom with a push of her flippers. Sand plumes trail from her 'flippertips', as she swims slowly but steadily for deeper water. The baby takes up his station behind her flipper, stroking rapidly with its tail to keep up. Occasionally he can coast a bit on the pressure wave created by his mother. There is a constant duet of squeaks between the two, reassuring each other that they are close together in face of the perceived threat. The manatee's only defense is to flee. The swimmers are not daunted, one chases after the mother and calf until outdistanced, while the others look for other manatees to touch.

The mother knows another spot to stay warm about a mile (2 km) away. On their way to this new resting site, they stop to feed on a patch of *Hydrilla*. This is an exotic, invasive aquatic plant that was introduced into Crystal River probably as the result of someone dumping aquarium water into the river in the 1960s. *Hydrilla* is extremely prolific and ten years or so after it became established had almost choked the river. Each winter the manatees, along with cooler weather, would knock back the invasive plant to a manageable level. On the positive side, the manatees that came to Crystal River each winter loved to eat the plant so they had plentiful food where the water was warm. Sometimes they would literally eat their way through mats of vegetation, creating tunnels and underwater cathedrals of vegetation. In 1996, a storm hit the northwest coast of Florida and caused extensive flooding. Saltwater penetrated up the river to the headwaters and almost completely eradicated the salt-intolerant *Hydrilla*. When the plant nearly disappeared, an aggressive native alga erupted and covered most of the riverbed. Though manatees will eat algae from time to time, it is not particularly nutritious or preferred. It may take years for the other aquatic plants, preferred by manatees, to become established again in the river.

The noise of motorboats is overwhelming to the calf. They seem to be everywhere and each one

A minority of manatees are tame and allow themselves to be petted and stroked. This is an exciting experience for people, but may, in some instances, be illegal, as manatees are a highly protected species. It is important for people to be aware of the rules governing observing and touching manatees. It is far better to observe manatees from a distance for an opportunity to see a variety of natural behaviors, rather than the learned response of being petted.

sounds like it is approaching from a different direction. The first cold front of the season is known by all manatee lovers and divers to drive manatees into the clear waters of Crystal River. About 100,000 people come to Crystal River each winter to see and touch the manatees. Flotillas of boats converge on the river the first cold day, and every weekend in the winter the river is flooded with divers. The calf is confused by the boat sounds and stays close to his mother, who seems to be unperturbed by it all and continues to feed as the boats pass nearby and even overhead. She knows by the lower-frequency

sound emitted by the slower RPM of the engines that these boats are of little threat and that she can avoid them if necessary.

By afternoon, they have arrived at the other small spring about half a mile up a canal. This spring has been roped off as a manatee sanctuary, forming a box about 65 ft (20 m) long and 30 ft (10 m) wide. Manatees are stacked like cordwood in this postage-stamp refuge. Most of them are sleeping quietly, sometimes lying one or two deep inside the boundaries of the refuge, with hordes of divers just outside the rope barriers peering at them. When one or two manatees become hungry, they venture out of the refuge, running the gauntlet of people wanting to touch a manatee.

As night falls and after the divers have left, the two also move out of the refuge and roam the river looking for food in several choice spots that the mother remembers. They also travel halfway down the river to feed on beds of their favorite food, shoal grass. But down the river, the water is cold, so they don't linger more than an hour before they head back upstream to get warm again. This time they head straight for the refuge and spring. This feeding pattern and the shifting back and forth between springs and sanctuaries will continue throughout the winter. The calf will grow quickly and will begin venturing further and further away from his mother. He will interact with other manatees, particularly calves and juveniles, by rolling, touching and cavorting. The female will tend to remain solitary with the exception of her calf and the occasional young male that may accompany her from a few hours to days.

By the end of February, the Gulf temperature is approaching the temperature of the spring waters. Many of the manatees have already left the river for other areas. If a late season cold snap occurs, they will find the closest warm water source for temporary shelter. It can be another spring, effluent from a power plant or even a deep canal that, because of its depth, will not change temperature rapidly. Tia is getting anxious to leave and is making longer forays down the river. Even though the temperature of the spring is warm relative to Gulf waters during the winter, 73°F (23°C) is still below the optimal comfort level for this tropical species. Water temperatures in the mid to high twenty degrees Celsius would be preferable. She waits for the temperature of the Gulf to warm above the spring temperature to depart Crystal River and head for her preferred summer area of East Pass, where there are the lush beds of shoal grass waiting.

In the first week of March the conditions are right and they both leave the river and head north along the coast through the labyrinth of oyster beds. Sometimes the water is so shallow in these coastal areas that the sharp edges of the oysters cut their bellies as they pass over them, leaving characteristic scars. When they reach the mouth of the Withlacoochee River they linger for a few days, feeding around the mouth of the river on Widgeon Grass, another preferred food, and take in fresh water. Turning northwest they make the day journey across the open Gulf to Cedar Keys a few kilometers east of East Pass. As during their journey down, the calf continually takes in the tastes, sounds and, when possible, visual landmarks of their passage. This way he creates a sensory roadmap of the route.

The calf is quite large now. He feeds equally on mother's milk and on vegetation. He explores much of the surrounding area alone, staying within auditory range of his mother. He has learned through several close encounters with fast boats to recognize the characteristic high-frequency sounds they emit. He has learned how to react by following the movements and response of his

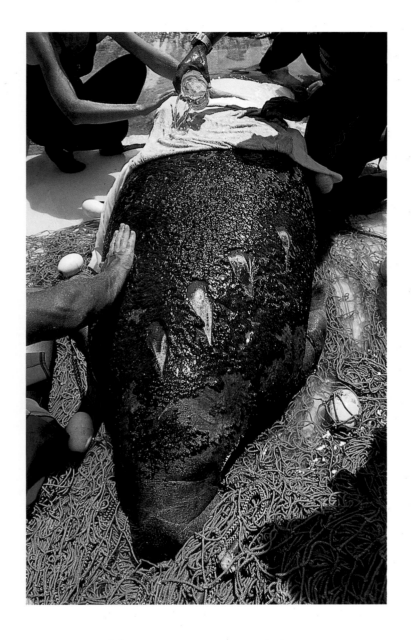

A manatee is rescued after suffering multiple lacerations caused by a collision with a motorboat (left). Over 25 percent of the manatee carcasses retrieved in Florida are deaths caused by watercraft. Each year 15 to 20 manatees are rescued by government biologists and commercial aquarium facilities that take in the injured manatees for treatment (above). After recovery, and when possible, these manatees are released back into the wild. Wildlife Trust, a non-profit research and conservation organization, monitors many of these released manatees using satellite telemetry to help ensure their successful adaptation back into the wild. You can follow the movements of these manatees and receive weekly updates on the website: **www.wildtracks.org**

mother, who has survived so many strikes. He has learned to tuck and dive when a boat approaches or if the water is too shallow to dive, then to flee for the nearest deep channel to get away.

The summer is typical of the previous one and the calf continues to grow and become increasingly independent. In August, the two are feeding in shallow water on a particularly lush bed of seagrass just off the main boat channel at the mouth of the Suwannee River. Several fast recreational fishing boats speed out of the channel on their way to their favorite fishing grounds further offshore in the Gulf of Mexico. Though the passing sounds agitate the two manatees and they remain alert, they both continue their feeding activity off the boat channel. They have also learned that the boats tend to stay in the channel and avoid the shallow water along the edges. All is calm, and there are one or two other manatees feeding nearby.

The first signal of danger is the sound of water rushing and splashing nearby, but little else. It could be a brown pelican plunging after a school of fish. Suddenly the rushing sound and waves have become tremendously loud and are accompanied by an unusual high wine engine noise. The personal watercraft or jet-ski has been speeding along the edge of the channel at about 40 kts. It doesn't travel in a specific direction but races in a zig-zag pattern, circling around and sometimes spinning on its axis like a top. The jet-ski comes on them practically with no warning, so quickly that they have only one startled reaction — to flee as quickly as possible to the deepest water. In a giant froth of spray, waves and mud that erupts from their whipping tails and the pressure wave of their huge bodies pushing through the shallow water, mother and calf plow toward the channel, completely panicked by the sudden encounter. In their alarm and single-minded response to find deep water, they do not detect the 30 ft fishing boat with twin 250 hp outboards cruising at 25 kts back from a day's fishing in the Gulf. The skipper's attention is drawn toward the jet-ski nearby who has now stopped his speeding convolutions and is recovering and reflecting on his near encounter with the manatees he nearly hit. The fishing boat doesn't notice the two manatees only 30 yards (27 m or about 3 boat lengths) ahead of him; it takes his boat just 2.1 seconds to close the distance. The two outboards project down into the water about 3 ft (1 m).

At the last instant before impact, both manatees react simultaneously by tucking their heads and twisting away. The mother is struck first. She is hit by the lower unit or the metal covering of the drive shaft, which is narrow and shaped like a dagger. It strikes her perpendicularly between her flipper and her midsection. A large proportion of the energy and force of the boat is transferred to this narrow hunk of machinery slicing through the water. The force of the strike pushes her briefly through the water into her calf who dives for his life. The propeller of the second engine brushes the baby's back near its tail and cuts deep into the flesh, but misses severing his spine by a few centimeters. Though painful, his injury will heal and a wide gray scar will likely remain for the rest of his life. His mother is less lucky; though she has been hit once nearly every year of her life, in this 21st year she had become confused and couldn't get out of the way. The blow does not have the characteristic parallel scars of the propeller, in fact there is only a superficial cut on her side. But during a necropsy one would see how several ribs were shattered and punctured her lungs.

She probably did not die immediately, but languished for hours or a day while air escaped into her body cavity, called a pneumothorax. Manatee biologists, since they see so many manatees in this condition, call them 'bobbers' because it is difficult for them to submerge. If an injured manatee is sighted, the report is given to Florida wildlife authorities who quickly gather a trained team to capture the animal. Rescued manatees are taken to one of several commercial aquaria in Florida where they receive medical treatment and are sometimes, after recovery, released back out into the wild. Often they die and the carcasses are retrieved and taken to the Florida Fish & Wildlife Conservation Commission (FWC) where thorough necropsies are performed to determine the cause of death.

Unfortunately, the year ends tragically for Tia. Her calf is old enough to make it on his own and he will have learned from this painful experience. Hopefully, he remembers enough from his earlier journey with his mother and perhaps he can take up with another manatee or two to find his way back to Crystal River when the first cold front arrives. This sad story occurs every week in Florida, as over 80 manatees a year killed by boat strikes are recovered by the FWC. This statistic does not even consider the suffering and injuries caused by the multiple strikes and lacerations that the manatees are subjected to each year.

Conservation

Sirenians are legally protected practically everywhere they are found. Manatees in Florida have been protected by Florida state law since the nineteenth century when hunting was considered a major threat. Today manatees are protected by the Florida Sanctuary Act of 1978 and also two U.S. federal statutes, the Endangered Species Act and the Marine Mammal Protection Act. Hunting poses less of a problem for the Florida manatee today; instead most manatee deaths occur due to collisions with motorboats, entanglement in fishing gear, ingestion of hooks and other discarded trash and drowning in automatic flood control structures. For example in 2001, 325 manatee carcasses were recovered in Florida. Of these, 81 (25 per cent) were killed by watercraft, one died in a flood control structure and 8 died from other human related causes. The proportion of manatees killed by watercraft in 2001 was similar to recent years, but 2001 was the highest year on record for overall manatee deaths. Scientists are concerned that this level of mortality cannot be sustained.

Several areas of the state have shown increases in manatee numbers over the past twenty years, such as the Crystal River on the west coast of Florida and Blue Springs region on the St. Johns River. Together, these two areas contain less than 20 per cent of Florida's manatee population. These two regions have had manatee protective measures in place for over 20 years such as, regulating boat speeds and providing sanctuaries that limit human disturbance and protection of manatee habitat. In other areas of Florida, the waterways are becoming increasingly congested and coastal human population growth is rapid. In these areas, where it is much less certain that manatee population growth is continuing, the prospect for manatee long term survival is uncertain. Manatee population models and projections indicate that numbers are stable or slightly increasing, but it is likely that population declines will occur if mortality continues to increase. We also know that the basis for some of the models are from aerial survey data that show considerable variation based on survey conditions and the fact that methods and effort have changed over the past 20 years.

These scientific models do not attempt to account for what will happen to manatee populations as coastal habitats are altered due to ever-increasing coastal development and human population growth. Where will manatees go if sources of warm water are lost when future power plants are built using closed cooling systems, or if these facilities move inland because of rising market costs and regulatory conditions? Natural sources of warm water such as springs are also at risk. Water demand in Florida from agriculture, municipal use and watering golf courses, along with lingering drought conditions is outstripping recharging of the underground aquifer. Consequently, water levels and flow are decreasing. Many springs are drying up and others are suffering diminished flow.

You can often hear fishermen say, 'I see more manatees now than ever before.' This is testament that manatee populations in Florida have been recovering from levels that were once lower. Scientists believe that manatee populations have been slowly growing since probably their lowest levels at the turn of the twentieth century. Manatee populations in Florida may have suffered serious setbacks due to unusual and extended cold temperatures before the introduction of artificially heated water and population levels may have remain depressed due to hunting, particularly around clear springs such as Manatee Springs. It was not until 1893 that legislative action protected the species from hunting, after which their numbers began to slowly increase.

Hunting can be relatively easily restricted and regulated. The new threats to manatees, such as boat-related deaths and habitat change, are more difficult for wildlife managers to address and will worsen with continued development and growth. Efforts to regulate boat speeds have been met with considerable opposition, including legal challenges by those that feel their individual rights are being curtailed to have free and convenient access to waterways. When once there was open dialog and discussion between boaters, fisherman and those that enjoy and understand manatees about how best to protect the species, now there is 'management by lawsuit' with decisions being made by courts and lawyers rather than scientists, wildlife managers and stakeholders. This polarization among groups is difficult to correct and may continue to worsen and result in changes to management actions that could reverse positive manatee population growth trends. Changes in management direction at this juncture, before human-related threats to the species are under control now and into the future, would be tragic.

Outside the U.S., manatees and dugongs are hunted throughout their range. In some parts of their range, dugongs have been commercially exploited, as were Amazonian manatees, with thousands being harvested for meat; manatee and dugong meat is still sold openly in some world markets. In Australia, dugongs are legally protected but can be taken by aboriginal hunters in specific areas. Though manatees are also protected throughout the regions they inhabit, hunting often takes place with the knowledge of local authorities. In West Africa, for example, certain festivities are annually celebrated with the killing, roasting and partaking of manatee meat – with the invited participation of (and enjoyment by) local dignitaries and authorities.

In Australia, dugongs are incidentally killed in shark nets that are set along popular beaches to protect swimmers. They are also killed, as are manatees, in nets set to catch sea turtles. Dugongs are vulnerable to oil spills; such was the case in 1983 when many dugongs died after the Nowruz oil spill in the Persian Gulf, and also after oil spills during the Gulf War. Oil spills have not, so far, proved particularly lethal to manatees. Manatees are incidentally killed in a variety of nets, weirs and structures.

Fishermen and hunters use a remarkable assortment of methods, not to mention ingenuity, in catching and killing manatees. In Africa, where they are prized for their meat and oil, specialized nets are frequently used to catch them. These nets have large mesh, big enough for the animal to enter but not wide enough for them to pass through. They become trapped in the mesh at the widest point of their body and entangled when they use their flippers to try and back out of the net. Several types of traps are also used. Another method is to construct modified corrals made of sticks stuck in the bottom lashed together to form a semi-circular fence. The open end has a sliding door resembling a giant box trap. The traps, baited with cassava, are constructed where manatees are known to feed or travel. When a manatee enters the trap, it trips a trigger stick, causing the door to fall and trapping the manatee inside the corral. Other techniques include fishermen baiting large shark hooks with cassava and attaching these to tethered floats. Manatees bite the cassava and become hooked. When the fishermen find the float and manatee, it is dispatched by harpoon, the weapon of choice for catching both manatees and dugongs. Most often the harpoon is constructed of a long pole with a detachable barbed head. The point

Hunting of manatees and dugongs remains a major threat in many areas where they are found. They are often considered a delicacy and an important source of meat in protein-deficient coastal regions. In some areas of Australia, where dugong numbers allow, regulated hunting by aboriginal people is permissible.

is tethered to a float. After the animal is struck with the harpoon, the head comes off and the sea cow pulls the float along until it tires. It is repeatedly struck with harpoons until it succumbs. A specialized harpoon that has multiple points usually made of large nails lashed together is sometimes used for dugongs. Another way manatees are hunted in Africa is to suspend a harpoon weighted by a log from an overhanging tree, or a special tower made of saplings stuck in the bottom. The weighted harpoon is set as a trap, so when the manatee tries to feed on a bait it tugs on a trigger cord that unleashes the suspended spear, which plunges into the head or back of the animal. Still another method is to build an elevated platform adjacent to a freshwater seep or source of food. When the manatee comes near, it is harpooned from the platform.

A tribute to manatees in the main spring of Crystal River.

In Africa, manatees have been killed by being sucked into turbines of hydro-electric dams. Each dry season, water levels in some rivers drop rapidly, causing manatees to become trapped in pools or lakes that communicate with major rivers when water levels are higher. Consequently every year many manatees become trapped in these temporary sanctuaries. In Nigeria, manatees move from the Benue River to the Pandam Lake to pass the dry season. In fact, Pandam Lake has been declared a manatee sanctuary. In other areas of West Africa, for example in Senegal, manatees become trapped in temporary lakes and each year wildlife officials transport a few back to the main river. In other places, manatees are not quite so fortunate; in Chad, fishermen opportunistically kill manatees when they find them stranded during the dry season.

Habitat changes pose one of the most serious threats to sirenians. In Africa, damming of rivers and cutting of mangroves in many areas may reduce food availability. When manatees become trapped behind dams, they may be killed by the operations of locks, flood gates or hydroelectric turbines. As well, during seasonal draw-downs of the lake, particularly during drought conditions, food may become limited since much of the vegetation that manatees utilize in Africa is bank growth. As the water recedes from the shore, with the draw-down of the lake, they are no longer able to reach their food.

Sirenians must also contend with many natural threats. Predation is uncommon, though there are occasional reports of sharks or crocodilians attacking calves or sometimes adults. Tiger shark attacks on dugongs have been reported from western Australia and killer whales may also feed on dugongs in rare instances.

Manatees can become debilitated and die from brevetoxins (red tide). Diseases are unusual in sirenians, in fact they appear to be remarkably disease free. They do succumb to secondary infections resulting from injuries and form reduced immune function due to cold stress. Scientists are concerned that during winter aggregations, when hundreds of manatees are in close quarters, the high density of manatees may make them particularly vulnerable to an emerging and contagious disease.

Will they survive? Sirenians have persisted for a million years or more. Their species diversity was once much greater than it is today, but what they lack in diversity may be compensated, to some degree, by the fact that the four remaining species of sea cows have a wide tropical distribution. The extant sirenians are generalists, that is, they are able to feed on a wide variety of foods and live in many types of habitats, from isolated lakes of the inland delta of Mali to strictly marine habitats of Puerto Rico. Within their range, they are found in practically every other marine, coastal or riverine habitat in between. In Florida, manatees have been described as an 'urban' species, certainly not in the sense that they have invaded urban areas, but because coastal development has encroached on their remaining habitat. They are commonly seen passing through the Miami River, or feeding on lawn grass along a canal used for irrigating a golf course. Sometimes they penetrate many kilometers up storm drains right into the heart of a metropolitan area. Once in the pipe, the animal cannot turn around, so it just follows the culvert until it ends or until the water is too shallow to continue. There it either dies or is rescued.

This is usually a major local event as various government officials, the press and crane operators converge to pull the beast out through a manhole.

Sea cows are robust, adaptable and persistent in the face of human-induced change. Individually they are tough. Manatees, for example, persevere against the odds when they suffer such traumatic and debilitating injury caused by powerboats practically on an annual basis. We frequently discuss manatee survival in terms of population growth and mortality levels, but we seldom consider the suffering individuals must endure when they are hit by boats. How does this stress and the physiological demands required for healing affect reproduction and ability to raise calves? One female manatee was hit at least 49 times by powerboats. We know this, because the 50th boat strike killed her and scientists at the FWC's Florida Marine Research Institute (FMRI), who conduct necropsies on practically every manatee carcass recovered in Florida, were able to accurately measure and catalog the scars from each previous boat strike. Sadly, this is the fate of many manatees.

Simple math tells us that when manatee deaths exceed births for any extended period of time then the population will begin to decline. Obviously, if the overall population is larger, then the time it takes for the population to decline toward extinction will be longer than if the population is smaller. Disturbing information from aging of carcasses has recently come to light from the work of Megan Pitchford at FMRI. Every manatee carcass recovered in Florida is aged by counting the annual growth rings of their ear bones. Based on a collection of over 3000 ear bones, she has determined that even though manatees can live to 50 years or more, females do not usually survive much longer than seven years. The age of sexual maturity is around five years, so females often do not have a chance to reproduce more than once or twice before they are killed. The manatee's slow reproductive rate of a calf about every 2½ years makes them particularly vulnerable to high mortality. If females are not able to live out their lives or their 'reproductive potential' because of human-induced mortality, then this puts the population further at risk, particularly if the age structure declines towards younger animals that do not live long enough to reproduce more than once or twice. We also believe that calves learn many of their behaviors from their mothers, such as finding warm water, how to

Two manatees from Crystal River,
identified by scars remaining from
encounters with powerboats. Both of
these animals are known to me from
the late 1960s and early 1970s. These
old acquaintances have continued to
use Crystal River as their winter home
for over 30 years.

A pair of manatees surface together as they often do, touching muzzle to muzzle as they breathe.

navigate waterways, where to find food, how to avoid boats. Like elephants who teach their young where to find limited resources during lean years, manatees probably obtain this type of knowledge as well. Older females become a source of knowledge that can be transferred through experience to their offspring. Manatees need to know where to go and what to do when resources such as springs dry up, power plants shut down or seagrass is uprooted by storms. If mothers are getting younger and have not previously experienced these 'bad years', then much of this knowledge and tradition may be lost and cannot be taught to their offspring. We also know that younger and inexperienced mothers are not as successful in raising offspring. This may help to partially explain rising newborn manatee deaths.

The increasing population of manatees in the United States since the turn of the century is remarkable. It certainly can be partially attributed to many factors, such as the introduction of aquatic weeds that have increased their food resources and the construction of power plants that have increased the availability of warm water, enabling the species to expand their winter range. Ultimately the success can be attributed to an expansive and comprehensive conservation effort that has, for now, balanced the impact of burgeoning human population growth in Florida and consequent cumulative impacts of coastal development.

If we look backward, we can be optimistic. If we look forward we may feel a little less secure. It may well be that we will reflect back on the 'good ole days' of the twentieth century when the issues were less complex and contentious. During the last century regulating hunting and controlling boat speeds to reduce mortality when there was little resistance may have been relatively easy and certainly seems to have been effective in most areas of Florida. Today, in the early twenty-first century, as a consequence of perceived infringement of 'personal rights', there is growing opposition to regulatory actions aimed at being proactive, such as creating boat speed zones where no mortality has necessarily occurred but where the probability of a manatee/boat collision is great, such as near inlets or narrow canals that join waterways. It is more difficult for management to take a strong stance and win over public support when the 'numbers' of manatees have been increasing. But the fact is that using numbers alone doesn't tell biologists and managers what they need to know about the population to best determine its health or prescribe a solution. In short, population numbers alone do not contain the critical information needed to determine if a species can survive. For example, a population number does not tell us:

1) the reproductive potential – if there are more females than males or females at reproduction age

2) the impact of mortality on the population

3) what proportion of the population survives from one year to the next

4) the age structure - if there is a disproportionate number that are young or very old – information which is critical to determining the success of a population

For all these reasons and others, we don't consider a number used alone to be useful in predicting future survival. It is the ratio of births to deaths, the age structure of the population and adult survival that are the most important demographics, but the real test is to estimate the impacts of future threats to survival – such as habitat loss, increasing boat traffic, loss of seagrass beds, and catastrophic events like a cold front or red tide.

Around the world, sirenians are enjoying a higher profile and increased interest by the public and scientific community. More and more sirenian research and conservation efforts are emerging. In conjunction, there are more protected areas and economic incentives for their conservation. Manatee viewing as a source of eco-tourism is developing in many areas outside of Florida, particularly Belize, Brazil and Costa Rica. Given half a chance, like the situation we have seen in Florida over the past half century, manatees and their brethren the dugong can survive and their numbers can increase. The challenge is to look forward and remember that this unique group of animals are slow to reproduce and can only recover their numbers very slowly. Managers cannot relax conservation strategies until future threats and habitats are under control and secure. We cannot wait for the day when that same fishermen mentioned in the beginning of this chapter, notices that he 'doesn't seem to see as many manatees as he used to'. By that time, when it is noticeable to the occasional fisherman, manatee population numbers will have slipped too far down the slippery slope toward extinction that recovery becomes difficult or impossible in the face of increasing future threats.

Manatee and Dugong Distribution Map

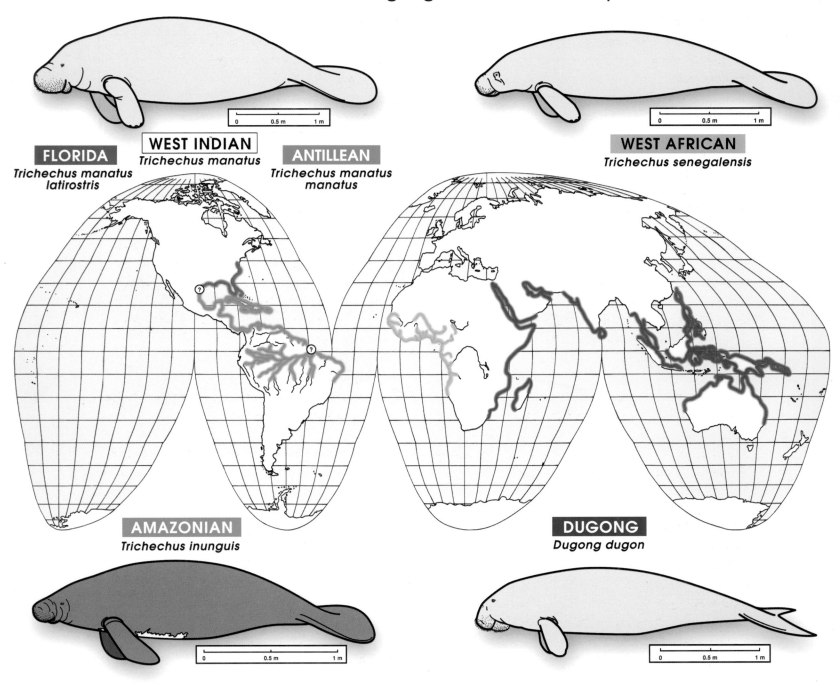

FLORIDA
Trichechus manatus latirostris

WEST INDIAN
Trichechus manatus

ANTILLEAN
Trichechus manatus manatus

WEST AFRICAN
Trichechus senegalensis

AMAZONIAN
Trichechus inunguis

DUGONG
Dugong dugon

Manatee and Dugong Facts

West Indian Manatee

Common names: Manatee; Sea Cow; Lamantin des Carabes; Vaca marina del Caribe

Scientific name: *Trichechus manatus*

Two subspecies: Florida manatee *Trichechus manatus latirostris*; Antillean manatee *Trichechus manatus manatus*

Gestation: 12-14 months

Age at maturity: 4-5 years

Longevity: probably 60-70 years

Adult weight: 3085 lb (1400 kg)

Max. known total lengths: male 12 ft (3.7 m), female 13 ft 6 inches (4.1 m)

Color: Gray, brown or even greenish depending on types of algae growing on the skin

Distinguishing characteristics: Completely aquatic, broad back, no dorsal fin, nostrils located on tip of snout, round tail, fingernails on the tips of foreflippers, rough skin with sparse hairs, no markings unless scarred from injuries caused by watercraft collisions.

Amazonian Manatee

Common names: Manatee; Sea Cow; Peixe-boi; Lamantin de l'Amazonie; Vaca marina del Amazon

Scientific name: *Trichechus inunguis*

Gestation: About 12 months

Age at first reproduction: 4-6 years

Longevity: Probably more than 60 years

Adult weight: 1102 lb (500 kg)

Total length: 9 ft (2.8 m)

Color: Dark gray to black with white or pinkish blazes on the ventral surface.

Distinguishing characteristics: Completely aquatic, broad back, no dorsal fin, nostrils located on tip of snout, round tail, no fingernails on the tips of foreflippers, smooth skin with sparse hairs.

West African Manatee

Common names: Manatee; Sea Cow; Lamantin

Scientific name: *Trichechus senegalensis*

Gestation: probably 12-14 months

Age at maturity: probably 4-5 years

Longevity: probably 60-70 years

Adult weight: unknown, probably around 2204 lb (1000 kg)

Max. known total lengths: male 10 ft 10 inches (3.3. m), female 9 ft 10 inches (3 m)

Color: Dark gray to brown depending upon types of algae growing on the back.

Distinguishing characteristics: Completely aquatic, broad back, no dorsal fin, nostrils located on tip of snout, round tail, fingernails on the tips of foreflippers, rough skin with sparse hairs.

More slender with a blunter snout than West Indian manatee.

Dugong

Common names: Dugong; Sea Cow; Dugong; Sea Pig

Scientific name: *Dugong dugon*

Gestation: 13-14 months

Age at first reproduction: 6 years, but may not give birth until 10 - 17 years

Longevity: 70+ years

Adult weight: 2204 lb (1000 kg)

Max. recorded total length: 13 ft 6 inches (4.1 m)

Color: Brownish to gray skin

Distinguishing characteristics: Smooth skin covered with sparse hairs, no dorsal fin, fluked tail with laterally compressed caudal peduncle, nostrils located on tip of snout.

Males and rarely females have two large incisors (tusks) not visible when the mouth is closed.

Index

*Entries in **bold** indicate pictures*

Recommended Reading

Bryden, Michael et al. *Dugongs, Whales, Dolphins, and Seals: A guide to the Sea Mammals of Australasia.* St. Leonards: Allen & Unwin, 1998.

Reynolds, John E. III and Daniel K. Odell. *Manatees and Dugongs.* New York: Facts on File, 1992.

Lefebvre, L.W., T.J. O'Shea, G.B. Rathbun and R.C. Best. *Distribution, status, and biogeography of the West Indian manatee.* pp. 567-610. Biogeography of the West Indies, ed. C.A. Woods. Gainesville, Fl. Sandhill Crane Press. 1989.

Reynolds, J.E. III, and J.R. Wilcox. *People, powerplants, and manatees.* Sea Frontiers 33(4): 263-269. 1987.

Hartman, D.S.. *Ecology and behavior of the manatee* (Trichechus manatus) in Florida. Special publication no. 5, American Society of Mammalogists. 1979.

Reynolds, J.E. III. *The semisocial manatee.* Natural History. 88(2): 44-53. 1979.

Powell, J.A., *The distribution and biology of the West African manatee* (Trichechus senegalensis). Unpub. Contract Report UN Environmental Program. 1996.

Timm, R.M., L. Albuja V. and B.L. Clauson. *Ecology, distribution, harvest, and conservation of the Amazonian manatee Trichechus inunguis in Ecuador.* Biotropica 18(2): 150-156. 1986.

Ridgway, S.H. and R. Harrison (editors). *The Sirenians and Baleen Whales. Handbook of Marine Mammals.* Vol. 3. Academic Press, New York. 1985.

Smith, A., and H. Marsh. *Management of traditional hunting of dugongs* (Dugong dugon) *in the northern Great Barrier Reef, Australia.* Environmental Management 14(1):47-55. 1990.

Marsh, H., H. Penrose, C. Eros, and J. Hugues. *Dugong: Status reports and action plans for countries and territories.* UNEP Early Warning and Assessment Report Series. 2002.

US Fish & Wildlife Service. *Florida manatee* (Trichechus manatus latirostris) *recovery plan, 3rd revision.* US Fish & Wildlife Service, Atlanta, Ga. USA. 2002

Biographical Note

Dr. James Powell has studied manatees for over 30 years in Florida, Africa and the Caribbean. He is co-chair of the IUCN Sirenia Specialist Group and is author of many articles and publications on sirenians. He was formerly the coordinator for the state of Florida's research program on manatees and currently is the Director for Aquatic Conservation for Wildlife Trust, a non-profit research and conservation organization based in New York.